Advance praise for
IF THEY COME FOR US

"Fatimah Asghar's *If They Come for Us* is a beautiful book of poems that, as powerfully and deeply as any book I've read in a good while, wonders about, explores and laments our many inheritances of violence, which are also inheritances of sorrow, and the ways those inheritances reside in our bodies and imaginations. The ways those inheritances, in fact, structure our bodies and imaginations. And yet, the wonder of this book is the way that throughout the anguish and sorrow and rage, despite it, there is tenderness. There is sweetness. There is care. This book reminds us: These, too, are our inheritances. These, too, are our heirlooms. These, too, we must pass along."

—ROSS GAY, author of *Catalog of Unabashed Gratitude*,
winner of the 2015 National Book Critics Circle Award
and finalist for the 2015 National Book Award in Poetry

"I have never read a book that made me want to eat, write, revise, and love my body as much as *If They Come for Us* by Fatimah Asghar. This book gutted, cradled, and inspired me. Asghar's work isn't simply some of the most innovative work I've read; page after page, the book weaves productive ambiguity, textured explorations of the body, and lyrical precision into a work that is somehow just as much a mammoth book of short stories, an experimental novel, and a soulful memoir. I'm not sure this nation is deserving of such a marvelous, sensual, and sensory book, but I know we needed this. We so needed this."

—KIESE LAYMON, author of *How to Slowly Kill
Yourself and Others in America* and *Long Division*

"In the title poem of *If They Come For Us*, Fatimah Asghar writes, 'my people / my people I can't be lost,' a statement that is as much a call to arms as it is a fervent plea. After reading Asghar's widely anticipated debut collection, I not only believed her, but began to feel that all of us could be as sacred, protected, and celebrated by looking to each other's stories and considering them alongside our own. In poems that are as historically aware as they are forward-thinking, Asghar reminds us with wit, wisdom, and compassion that a truly felt and thoughtfully written poem can be many things at once: a salve, an artifact, a talisman, and a flashlight in the face of imminent darkness. This book is a brightness that will carry you as you carry it with you."

—TARFIA FAIZULLAH, author of *Registers of Illuminated Villages* and *Seam*

"With breathtaking intelligence and care, Fatimah Asghar writes enduring poems that, from varied angles, investigate the histories and resonances of the Partition across the lives of her subjects. Her vision is attuned to the peripheries, is diasporic, and, thus, steeped in loss, simultaneities, invention. Part of the strength and vulnerability of this work is rooted in what I'm thinking of as a *poetics of or*. Asghar does not fix or flatten her subjects, but rather, engages each poem as at least one of several imaginative routes through which she/we might engage history and possibility. In this way, these poems bend time, encircle kin, invent new forms of saying. They laugh, lose, and lament, challenging language even as they are led by it: 'Allah, you gave us a language / where yesterday & tomorrow / are the same word. Kal. [. . .] Tomorrow means I might // have her forever. Yesterday means / I say goodbye, again.' But my chest bursts most with Ashgar's ability to render the fullness of life and human effort with the tiniest of details: mehndi on fingers, blisters on the back of a heel, laughter as a way of letting someone know you're still there. I leave these poems so deeply moved by her keen observations of the ephemeral. Even as she mourns the world, there is such fierce, resilient awe everywhere here. Such poems embolden me into love and dreaming and action."

—ARACELIS GIRMAY, author of *Kingdom Animalia* and *The Black M*

If They Come for Us

IF THEY COME FOR US

Poems

Fatimah Asghar

ONE WORLD
NEW YORK

Copyright © 2018 by Fatimah Asghar

Published in the United States by One World, an imprint of Random
House, a division of Penguin Random House LLC, New York.

ONE WORLD is a registered trademark and its colophon is a
trademark of Penguin Random House LLC.

ISBN 978-0-525-50978-3
Ebook ISBN 978-0-525-50979-0

Printed in the United States of America on acid-free paper

oneworldlit.com
randomhousebooks.com

9 8 7 6 5 4 3 2 1

FIRST EDITION

Book design by Simon M. Sullivan

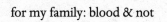

for my family: blood & not

"It's humiliating to wake up

alive, fifty years later, when I couldn't have saved you.
I couldn't have saved a dog."

Suji Kwock Kim

"They said, no, can these sorts of things ever happen?
I said to them if they have not happened before, they have happened
today."

Rajinder Singh, Partition survivor

Contents

At least 14 million people were forced into migration as they fled the ethnic cleansings and retributive genocides that consumed South Asia during the India/Pakistan Partition, which led to India's and East and West Pakistan's independence from colonial Britain. An estimated 1 to 2 million people died during the months encompassing Partition. An estimated 75,000 to 100,000 women were abducted and raped. Partition remains one of the largest forced migrations in human history; its effects and divisions echo to this day.

If They Come for Us

For Peshawar

DECEMBER 16, 2014

> *Before attacking schools in Pakistan, the Taliban sends kafan,*
> *a white cloth that marks Muslim burials, as a form of psychological terror.*

From the moment our babies are born
are we meant to lower them into the ground?

To dress them in white? They send flowers
before guns, thorns plucked from stem.

Every year I manage to live on this earth
I collect more questions than answers.

In my dreams, the children are still alive
at school. In my dreams they still play.

I wish them a mundane life.
Arguments with parents. Groundings.

Chasing a budding love around the playground.
Iced mango slices in the hot summer.

Lassi dripping from lips.
Fear of being unmarried. Hatred of the family

next door. Kheer at graduation. Fingers licked
with mehndi. Blisters on the back of a heel.

Loneliness in a bookstore. Gold chapals.
Red kurtas. Walking home, sun

at their backs. Searching the street
for a missing glove. Nothing glorious.

A life. Alive. I promise.

I didn't know I needed to worry
about them
until they were gone.

My uncle gifts me his earliest memory:
                    a parking lot full of corpses.

No kafan to hide their eyes
                    no white to return them to the ground.

In all our family histories, one wrong
                    turn & then, death. Violence

not an *over there* but a memory lurking
                    in our blood, waiting to rise.

We know this from our nests—
                    the bad men wanting to end us. Every year

we call them something new:
                    British. Sikhs. Hindus. Indians. Americans. Terrorists.

The dirge, our hearts, pounds vicious, as we prepare
                    the white linen, ready to wrap our bodies.

Partition

you're kashmiri until they burn your home. take your orchards. stake a
different flag. until no one remembers the road that brings you back.
you're indian until they draw a border through punjab. until the british
captains spit *paki* as they sip your chai, add so much foam you can't
taste home. you're seraiki until your mouth fills with english. you're
pakistani until your classmates ask what that is. then you're indian
again. or *some kind of spanish*. you speak a language until you don't.
until you only recognize it between your auntie's lips. your father was
fluent in four languages. you're illiterate in the tongues of your father.
your grandfather wrote persian poetry on glasses. maybe. you can't
remember. you made it up. someone lied. you're a daughter until they
bury your mother. until you're not invited to your father's funeral.
you're a virgin until you get too drunk. you're muslim until you're not
a virgin. you're pakistani until they start throwing acid. you're muslim
until it's too dangerous. you're safe until you're alone. you're american
until the towers fall. until there's a border on your back.

Kal

Allah, you gave us a language
where yesterday & tomorrow
are the same word. Kal.

A spell cast with the entire
mouth. Back of the throat
to teeth. Tomorrow means I might

have her forever. Yesterday means
I say goodbye, again.
Kal means they are the same.

I know you can bend time.
I am merely asking for what
is mine. Give me my mother for no

other reason than I deserve her.
If yesterday & tomorrow are the same
pluck the flower of my mother's body

from the soil. Kal means I'm in the crib,
eyelashes wet as she looks over me.
Kal means I'm on the bed,

crawling away from her, my father
back from work. Kal means she's
dancing at my wedding not-yet come.

Kal means she's oiling my hair
before the first day of school. Kal
means I wake to her strange voice

in the kitchen. Kal means
she's holding my unborn baby
in her arms, helping me pick a name.

When the Orders Came

> "[We are] calling for a total and complete shutdown of
> Muslims entering the United States."
> —Donald Trump's administrative team, December 7, 2015

they shipped us to the sanctuary camps
& we forgot our other countries.

like good schoolchildren we sang
the anthem loud, so loud
until we could hear nothing else.

not the birds delighting
over their young, or the dogs' snarl
at our feet, or him on the news

hourly, growling. this is the cost
of looking the other way
when they come for us.

I build safety inside you
& wake in cuffs.
I'm all mouth. every morning

I whisper *my country my country my country*
& my hands stay empty.
what is land but land? a camp

but a camp? sanctuary
but another grave? I am an architect.
I permission everything

into something new.
I build & build
& someone takes it away.

100 Words on 45's 100 Days

his last name means *to win;*

he drops bombs flattening

children to prove he can.

my friends write "not my president"

online. I am the farthest

from home I've been in a long time.

I write "I pledge no allegiance"

but children stay dead,

buried by cement in syria

or a cop's bullet in america

& he goes on golfing, vacationing,

his belt swelling past buckle

while swarms of children never grow

up. he's not my president but I live

in a country whose sun is war

we keep rotating around its warmth

our faces, sun-kissed, each & every morning.

How We Left: Film Treatment

[Establishing Shot]
Here's the image Auntie P gave me: the street a pool
of spilled light & all the neighborhood children
at my grandfather's knee. Kids: turbaned or taqiyahed
or tilakaad or not. How Jammu smelled of jasmine.

[Elevator Pitch]
Yes, I've heard your story—the man who saved my family
before they were my family. The boy who sat, crowned
at the cusp of my grandfather's light, who walked to their place
belt wrapped around books, swinging their shadows to the sun.

[Primary Research]
Ullu remembers it like this: clutching a suitcase of toys
when the men came, machetes swinging the sun red. The year
we found out who we were & who we were not. Muslims boarded
on the bus. Sikh men, laughing: *you wanted a fairytale & now you'll
    get it.*

[Rationale]
It takes a lot of work to remember we are nothing.
What has history given us but a fickle home? A legacy
of bloodied men. What's a nation to the sky? Some other wood
to call ours, some other snippet of cloud to pretend we own.

[Secondary Research]
My mom's clean, lean legs pounding the ground. Kirpans
catching light, limbs lost in long grass. Her hand above, searching
for someone's to hold. The red rain falling on the leaves.
The ground: a rose river begging her to swim.

[Working Title]
Pakistan: Disneyland, a fairytale promised. Land of prayer mats & ladoo.
Fat chum chums dripping with pink coconut syrup & all the rupees
to buy them. Land of jobs & tender lamb sliding off the bone. Land
of endless Ramzan's magrib & nights bouncing with mehndi-ed feet.

[Legal & Ethical Considerations]
History didn't give me a blueprint for loving you, but here I am,
70 years after you crossed a blood-sodden field, building your altar.
History didn't give you a blueprint for loving us, but there you were,
guiding through the tall grass, kirpan clearing a red path.

[Character Breakdown]
They aren't soldiers. Just men. Men who wear matching shirts.
Men who carry machetes. Men who march in formation.
These aren't refugees, just families vacationing to the Promised Land.
We aren't at war. Just neighbors who like to kill each other.

[Sample Dialogue]
I know that man—my teacher—this bus goes right—right—left
—did you pack the attah—we'll come back when—yes—Kashmir
is our—what's a home anyway—I know that man—a prick at the wheel,
golden thread—bus gone left—you wanted a fairytale & now—

[Audio Element: Silence]
Auntie P talks of the apple orchards. The fruit piled into her arms.
Backyard's blossoms perfuming the whole neighborhood.
& my grandfather, yes, she loves the story of my grandfather, teaching
the neighborhood children while all the streetlights fireflyed the night.

[Constraints]
Even with all this light, I can't see past the silence of my family.
The silence of a home I've never lived in, the sins of a people mine
& also not mine. My aunt's long stare, Ullu's bowed eyes.
His voice's rough engine stalled in the blood-soaked mud.

[Contingency]
I'm a bad researcher: I don't know your name, what you did
other than take my family off the bus once we arrived at the park
-ing lot full of death. This is a love letter, I think. You're a murderer
I think. Did you save us, walk back & slaughter the rest?

[Target Audience]
Everyone wants Kashmir but no one wants Kashmiris.
Aren't I a miracle? A seed that survived the slaughter & slaughters
to come. I think I believe in freedom I just don't know where it is.
I think I believe in home, I just don't know where to look.

[Narrative Device: Flash Forward]
In America they slaughtered a temple of Sikhs because they thought
them us. Here we all become towelheads, amorphous fears praying
to a brown god. Others that become others that look like others.
They don't know our history, its locked doors & heavy whispers.

[Narrative Device: Flashback]
Bring back the books: belted in your hand, swinging
their shadowed love across your body. You—a schoolboy
handsome, sucking a cigarette, never worrying about your lungs
or gut—old man fears hanging on some distant clothesline.

[Visual Element: Filtered Light]
Ullu remembers it like this: the bus turning left. Right. Left?
The lot of parked busses, mountains of Muslims stacked to the sky.
A brown shirt & red crusted blade, running to them. My grandfather's
eyes wide: the boy who used to sit by his knee, now a man.

[Visual Element: Camera Swing]
You're the god of small slaughters. I'll write to you forever.
The man who would not let his teacher die. What stories
were your family told? Are your grandchildren in Jammu still,
throwing rocks at the armies who stain the streets?

[Property Rights]
Everyone wants Kashmir, a useless crown, a ruby fed blood
carved by machete. The past is a land I do not know.
I love a man who saved my family by stealing our home.
I want a land that doesn't want me. I love a land that doesn't exist.

[Denouement]
The image Ullu gave me: the long march through the forest
after, his mother's plea to Allah piercing the trees like a strangled bird.
My mother's eyes blank, as he held her hand, his siblings' squeals drying
in their throats. & there in the horizon: a new country, a broken promise.

[End Credits]

In another life, could you have been my uncle, throwing me over
your shoulders when I was a baby? & when I grew up
I could have taught your children's children's children until
the streetlights came on, until our neighborhood crowded night.

Partition

1945: my grandfather steps
off a train in Jammu & Kashmir.
drinks pani from the Muslim fountain.
my grandfather teaches
all the children in his village.

there are men
who won't touch his hands,
afraid his Muslim blood dirty.
when he passes they bend
& pet the stray dogs instead.

—

1947: a Muslim man sips whiskey
& creates a country.

Jinnah's photo framed & hung on the doors
of his believers.

freedom spat between every paan
-stained mouth as the colonizers leave

& the date trees dance
in Ramzan's winds.

—

1947: in fall the birds
fly south for safety
to hide from the cold.

1947: in fall my family flocks
south to Pakistan for safety
to hide from their neighbors.

—

1945: the allies open
the camps in Germany
& the photos roll into America.
the westerners end their war
& declare: never again.

—

1947: a man sees a girl
crying as she begs for water

he stares for a while & then
lights her on fire.

—

1946: a woman registers to vote
& then registers her grandmother,
long dead.

she casts a ballot for India to stay united
changes into her grandmother's
sari & casts the vote, again.

—

1947: the cannons sound during
Ramzan & everyone holds their breath

to find who survived. Laylat al-Qadr
births two new nations

no one knows the boundaries.
bodies spoon like commas, waiting

linking, waiting, linking.

—

2015: a Lahori naan seller
wakes to his old nightmare—

hacking a Sikh family to death.
he falls to his knees & pleads

Allah, forgive me. please forgive me.

—

1947: a woman washes the body
of a stranger lying on the street.

every dead woman blurs into another.
maybe she could be my sister she says

as she performs the ghusl, as her own
sister never returns home.

—

1943: famine spreads through
the British Raj.

in Bengal three million die
bones of skin, arms sharp as machetes.

—

1947: summer, in a Bihari marketplace
there's nothing but sag & edible flowers.

lines of people crowd the center.
their hands: empty.

—

1993: summer, in New York City
I am four, sitting in a patch of grass
by Pathmark.

an aunt teaches me how to tell
an edible flower
from a poisonous one.

just in case, I hear her say, *just in case.*

—

1947: a man attacks Jinnah on the street.
another man spits on Nehru.

my family died for your dream
they say.

bring me back my family.
bring me back my family.

—

1947: in Jammu the railway staff hose
blood off the platform.

it has been an unusual rain this year
they say, the bloodwater

spraying onto the grass. the stray dogs lay
about, bloated with flesh.

it has been an unusual rain this year
says a Muslim general, machete in his hand,

his troops surrounding a sleeping Hindu
village, as the sky above Rawalpindi wakes.

From

What They Say	How They Say It	What They Actually Mean
Where Are You From?	a short cut to the end, could be period. a lovesong if they weren't locking a drone on target.	you must not be from here. so, where are you from?
آپ کہاں سے ہیں؟	aap kahaa se hai?	there is a wrong answer
आप कहां से है?	aap kahaa se hai?	there is a wrong accent
تسیں کتھوں ہو؟	tusi kitho ho?	how did you forget? how will you remember?

Partition

Ullu partitions the apartment in two—
a thin blue wall cutting the deserted hall.
Toys & books on our side,

refrigerator, sink & TV with our Auntie A.
She sends us rations throughout the day & we stay
separate, not allowed to cross. I'm ten

& haven't been hugged in a long time.
Allah made a barrier between me & my mom.
Ullu makes a barrier between me & my aunt.

When he leaves we sit at the base of the blue wall
& I laugh loud so Auntie A knows
I'm alive & okay & she laughs loud so I know

she hasn't left & we sit like this for hours, hands
pressed to the felt, laughing, laughing
unable to see each other.

Portrait of My Father, Alive

at the pizza shop he eyes pepperoni
(pig sweats on everything here)

polka dot tie & pin-stripped suit childless
america's shiny windows glittering

he orders a slice with no sauce
no cheese no toppings *just the bread?*

just the bread he says & leaves
carrying his naan home.

Old Country

Old Country Buffet, where our family
went on the days we saved enough money.
Everyone was in a good mood, even Ullu—
our uncle who never smiled or took off his coat

& dyed his hair black every two weeks
so we couldn't tell how old he was. We marched
single file towards the gigantic red lettering
across the gravel parking lot to announce

our arrival. We, children carrying our rectangle
backpacks brimming with homework, calculators
& Lisa Frank trapper keepers, for we knew this was a day
without escape, spread out across all the booths

possible while our family ate & ate & snuck
food into the Tupperware they smuggled in
& no matter how we begged & whined
or the waitresses yelled or threatened to charge

us more money we weren't leaving
until my greedy ass family had their fill.
O, Old Country! The only place
we could get dessert & eat as much of it

as we wanted before our actual meal.
The only place we didn't have to eat all
the meat on our plates or else we were accused
of being wasteful, told our husbands

would have as many pimples as rice we left behind.
Here, our family reveled in the American
way of waste, manifest destinied our way
through the mac & cheese, & green bean

casseroles, mythical foods we had only
heard about on TV where American
children rolled their eyes in disgust. Here
we learned how to say *I too have had meat loaf*

& hate it, evidence we could bring back
to the lunch table as we guessed
what the other kids ate as they scoffed
at our biriyani. Here, the adults told

us if we didn't like the strawberry shortcake
we could eat the ice cream or jello we could
get a whole plate just to try a bite
to turn up our noses & that was fine.

Here we loosened the drawstrings
on our shalwaars & gained ten pounds.
Here we arrived at the beginning of lunch
hour & stayed until dinner approached

until they made us leave. Here we learned
how to be American & say:
we got the money

        we're here to stay.

Haram

"God supports my waxing habit."
—Khudejha Asghar

The day Auntie A saw my sister's pussy
hairs crawling out & around her underwear
so long that if you ripped through the tangles
you could part them into pigtails
was the day we were all given our own
pair of scissors & told to read namaaz.
Your hairiness is against Allah's will
my Auntie scolded, the disappointment
lined on her too-young face. The three
of us sisters lined up to wash our feet
in the tub, our shame quieting us as the wadu
water splashed all the way to our arms.
Khudejha had to do Astaghfirullah, repenting
for her evils as we cut each lock
of hair, discarding them in a plastic bag
we got from the corner store
because they were too thick to flush down
our struggling toilet. The next day, we sisters
woke at 5am to read the Qur'an,
massacring the scripture in our American
mouths. We read the Surah about not painting
your nails or altering any part of your body
& wondered about our sheared bushes,
once a part of us & now finding shelter
in some smelly garbage. Maybe we misunderstood

the Surah. Maybe we were outside Allah's creations.
But we knew better than to question my Auntie's law.
We speculated the Qur'an hadn't ever imagined
hairiness like ours, so vast, it was its own sin.

Playroom

I never had enough kens
so I made my barbies fuck
each other
or fuck beanie babies.

I never had more than one
beanie baby per species.
they were rarer
that way

& like some
perverted noah's ark
kept
from multiplying.

No one with skin
colored like theirs, *freaks*
like me. Lucky the barbies
needed their bodies.

I controlled
in my playroom.
Whole cities of beautiful
women, boundless

tits, fucking
sacks of animal. Plastic
legs thrusting until
the beanie said *yes*

balls
of beans spilling
to the floor. The ladies fucked
their corpses until Auntie A

made me throw them out.
Legions of identical
white women, skin glowing
like pearl milk, magnificent

as they stormed the gates
of the zoo
conquered each animal
one limb at a time.

Shadi

During Partition, 75,000 to 100,000 women were abducted and raped. Many of these women were forced to marry, or chose to stay with their abductors because they knew they would not be accepted back into the communities from which they had been stolen.

we've had our worth   told to us   since always:
          two goats   &   maybe a nose ring or bracelet.
                              we've tried to re-learn
            worth   outside our bodies   one day
may our names   come before   our sex

one day   may we be more   than a body
        may we forget   the threats   of our uncles
    selling us off   to some man   some round
belly & house   already brimming   with wives

may our names   come before   *you*
        come before   *butameez*   come before *whore*

may our silhouettes   not be followed
                    not be the last fed   & the first to wake
one day may   the men in our beds   not be strange

Boy

what do I do with the boy
who snuck his way inside
me on my childhood playground?

the day other kids shoved
my body into dirt & christened me
he appeared, *boy*, wicked

feral, swallowing my stride.
the boy who grows my beard
& slaps my face when I wax

my mustache. he was there too
the day on Ben's couch, wearing
my skirt, ranking the girls

in class. again, his legs slamming
concrete, my chest heaving
when we ran from cops

the night they busted the river party
again when I smashed the jellyfish
into the sand & grinded it down

to a pink useless pulp. together
we watched it throb, open & close
begging for wet. he was there.

I have a boy inside me & I don't know
how to tell people. like when
that man held me down & we said no.

& my boy, my lovely boy
he clawed & bit & cried just like
we were back on the dirt playground

scraped wrists & steady pounding
his eyes wide, until
he stopped making a sound.

Gazebo

One spring Ullu collected all the dead wood
he could find & built a gazebo. The brick backyard
pretended to be grass, all the pictures we took
from the waist-up for our Myspace pages
passing us off as suburban girls worthy of nature.
Our ironed hair, pressed straight down our backs
Claire's jewelry glinting in the sunlight. It wasn't long
before we started decorating the gazebo
with fake foliage. Painted leaves stapled to stem,
roses that never wilted. Actual flowers were expensive
& only for funerals. We had too many funerals to waste
flowers. But we loved our story: the gazebo
that dared to live on concrete. The plastic petals.
Always red. Always bright. Never in need of water.

Partition

It was 2000 & we knew nothing of history.
Just the shit we read in class about gods not ours.
It was all so simple then: Marilyn's Jamaican mom
told Ullu *we don't touch pork either.*
Their barbeques: an invitation, lines of jerk chicken

& goat smoldering on mid-summer lazy days
side by side with Ullu's garam masala kebabs.
Jaspreet's family was Punjabi too, from the other side
of Partition. All our food, shared & somewhat the same.
A different spice here & there, maybe

a different name, maybe their bread thicker or our daal
more red. In this new kingdom, children always lost
with no aptitude for maps or the lines the West drew in them.
When we went to Nabila's house we would all shout
Bangladesh! Bangladesh! All my people from Bangladesh!

Her mom's bewildered stare, our legs wiggling,
History paused, bodies slow-rolling like in the music videos
we devoured. We, children, bellowing our songs,
our names, our bodies stacked four to a bed
belonging, belonging, always, to each other.

To Prevent Hypothermia

After the race my teammates
kicked the boys off the bus
& into the downpour

blocked the windows
with their sweatshirts
peeled the wet clothes

from my skin, each inch
matted-down
disobedient, hair plastered

to my brown legs.
It took two hungry girls
to remove the spandex

from my paling thighs
their blonde hair a cascade
from heaven, water droplets falling

from their roots, stinging
my body. The ports tore
off my shirt & sports bra

my nipples lighthouses
in a swollen ocean, a trail
of dark hair running up

my belly. My whole boat
witness to my small naked frame
a gulf of shiver on the bus.

& their own hairless legs
disappearing into their shorts
skin ripe as peaches, reaching

for my brown body. These girls
who I had stolen glances at
while we changed & wished

I could look like. My locker
room crew. My 5am practice
girls. My lean over the starboard

side so she could pee off the rigor
girls. My two mile run after
eating *Annie's* mac-n-cheese girls.

They took turns rubbing life
back into my bones
offered clothes off their own

backs to keep me from shaking.
My girls, sandwiching me
in their heat until my joints

flowered, until the warmth
budded through my blood.
What more could I ask

than a team willing to undress
their captain, too cold
& rain-glittered to do it alone?

White Lie

Marilyn put me in all the lies to her parents.
The nights she snuck out with boys or to smoke
Black N Milds with her cousin Manny & his best
friend Malik. *Yes Mama Grace, we were watching Pokémon,*

*yes Mama Grace we watched it again, yes ma'am we really
do love that movie* threading whatever I could
into a cinematic re-creation while Marilyn beamed
bad-girl, gleaming, getting away with everything.

It wasn't long before Mia & Rachel put me in their lies
too, not that they even had anything to lie about.
It just felt good being able to lie & have a friend
no one suspected of treason. We were all virgins

& betted on who would lose it first. I was always last—
hairy, half-boy half-girl who got good grades
& could do no wrong. I never did anything
wrong. Not even when I let Anita's brother touch me

under the sheet when we watched movies. Or when
Jessica showed me her nipple rings during play
rehearsal & I stopped myself from licking them.
Or when I got so angry at my sister

I filed my nails to points & watched her sleep.
Or how when Aisha tried to commit suicide
I stopped talking to her. I was so much of a lie
I rewrote my family for anyone who listened:

yes, my father lives in Pakistan, a surgeon that stitches
hearts back together, my mother a pediatrician in
New York, auntie to all her patients & yes
of course they love me. But Boston

has better public schools & I get to see them
every holiday & we go on long drives
& talk about what I want to be when I grow
up & what they did when they were my age & how

they met & named me & are just so, so proud.

Oil

I'm young & no one around
                knows where my parents are from.

A map on our wall & I circle all
                the places I want to be. My Auntie A,

not-blood but could be,
                runs oil through my scalp.

Her fingers play the strands of my hair.
                The house smells like badam.

My Uncle Fuzzy, not-blood but could be,
                soaks them in a bowl of water.

My Auntie A says my people might
                be Afghani. I draw a ship on the map.

I write *Afghani* under its hull. I count
                all the oceans, blood & not-blood,

all the people I could be,
                the whole map, my mirror.

We got sent home early
& no one knew why. *I think we*
                are at war! I yelled to my sister
knapsacks ringing
                against our backs. I copy
-catted from Frances
                who whispered it when the teachers
got silent. Can't blame
                me for taking a good idea.
I collect words where I find them.

Two hours after the towers fell I crossed the ship
out on the map. I buried it under a casket of scribbles.

All the people I could be are dangerous.
The blood clotting, oil in my veins.

Someone wrote *anthrax* on my locker
where I keep my body mist. Alexandra
says I smell musty. All the boys laugh.
When was the last time you showered?

I did I did I did. I'm not I'm not I'm
not. I can make my own armor, oil all
the parts. IDid. ImNot. I can harden &
no one'll touch me. IDidImNot. I
laugh along. IDidImNot. I can't go to
my locker. ImNot. Can't see those
letters on metal. IDid. So I spray
myself with Marilyn's cucumber body
mist. IDidImNot. When I get home I'll
throw my clothes in the laundry again.
IDid. Find mice bites in my underwear.
ImNot. & tomorrow when I show up
none of the boys'll laugh.

The walk to school makes the oil pool on my forehead

a lake spilling under my armpits. The news said the oil's

drying up. America is starting wars to get it back. My people

are on the list. We can't survive without oil.

But, who's got money for both gas & lunch?

There's a rough spot above my ear where my head
wages war on itself. Thin skin, my doctor

says. But I stopped letting my Auntie A oil my hair.
My Auntie has a baby in her & I know

our pretend game is up. She's not my mother.
No one is. I have no blood. Just my body & all its oil.

The kids at school ask me where I'm from & I have no answer.

I'm a silent girl, a rig ready to blow. The towers fell two weeks

ago & I can't say blow out loud or everyone will hate me.

They all make English their own, say *that's the bomb*.

I know that word's not meant for me but I collect words

where I find them. I practice at night, the crater

it makes of my mouth. I whisper to my sheets

bombbombbombbombbombbombbombbombbombbombbombbombbomb

a little symphony, so round. I look up & make sure no one heard.

Land Where My Father Died

land of buildings & no good manners land of sunless people & offspring of colonizers land of no spice & small pox land of fake flowers land of shackle & branches made of rope land of wire fences grabbing sky land that mispronounces my grief land that skins my other land that laughs when my people die & paints targets on my future children's faces land that steals & says *mine* land that plants mines & says go back land that poisoned my mother & devoured her body land that makes my other language strange on my tongue land that stripped our saris & clips haloes to its flag land that eliminates cities land that says *home*land *security* land that built the first bomb & the last land that killed my father & then sent back his body land that made me orphan of thee I sing.

Lullaby

For Khudejha

when the sadness comes
my sister tells me a story—

a man buried in pakistan
a woman buried in new york city

when we sleep they wake
opposite sides of the world

the planet opens a tunnel
where they meet: dirt sky & worm

stars. the lovers dance,
all night, their way back

my father's fingertips
pressing against my mother's

crooked smile. her henna-dyed
hair light the underworld

the mole on his lip's left side
winks the dark.

The Last Summer of Innocence

was when the mosquito bites bloomed
across my ass, swells of mucus burst
when the bus bumped the way to school.

Blood seeping through the cotton
of my underwear. The wound
would dry, under-ripe blackberries, staining
the back of my dress. Each time I took my panties

off I tore the bites open. I went to the hospital
three times that summer, my body always leaking pus
slow dancing down the backs of my thighs
glistening like fresh baby oil in the moonlight.

The summer my sister shaved her armpits
even though the adults said she couldn't. She took
my uncle's dull razor & marveled at the smoothness
left our Muslim house in a long-sleeved shirt

before stripping down to a tube top on the bus.
Haram I hissed, but too wanted to be bare
armed & smooth, skin gentle & worthy
of touch. That was, until she had a lump

swell to the size of a golf ball from an ingrown hair
& we both landed back in the hospital room, doctors

vacuuming liquid out of our muscles. The last summer
of innocence was when my best friend

gave me the too-big thong with a silver heart clasp
& I put them on under my dress & buried my bloody
granny panties behind the bleachers in the soil the boys
used to touch each other & pretend it was a tackle.

The summer after the towers fell or were blown down
or up & I watched the TV over & over. The people
running from the fire & smoke & jumping
from the buildings, arms out like wings

their bird bodies orbiting the earth, a new sun.
It was the summer the TV told me I was dangerous
& I tried to learn Spanish so I could pretend
I was the other kind of other.

It was the days I memorized the green
leather seats of the school bus & stared
straight ahead when the popular girls asked
where I was from, my skin full of sores

pussing & oozing as the blood fled my body
trying to find anything else to call home.

Script for Child Services: A Floor Plan

Bedroom One
All orphans are raised by wolves. I called them sisters. We traveled as a pack: three to a bed, licking each other's fur. No one could hurt us.

Bedroom Two
I was young. I didn't know better. I was young. I lied it all away. I was young. The police were big. I was young. No one believe us. I was young. I was afraid. I was young. I made a mistake.

Living Room
Was I wrong then, for what I did? Was it betrayal or survival?

What's the difference?

Kitchen
Is this how you bend someone's mind to break? *Nothing happened.* We were wolves. They said we could survive anything.

Hallway
Forgive me Allah. I have always been wild. Still, I lie. My mistakes hang like a crescent bright in the sky.

Forgive me Allah. But I cant stop repeating. Nothing happened. Repeat after me:

Bathroom

The White House

or, off-white
beige even, at the edges
we couldn't clean

chipped porcelain tub
toilet that never flushed

where we hid
when Ullu was in a bad way
when we heard him slam

his feet up the stairs
his fists at the door

separating us
girls, elbowing each other
for a shot at safety

to be the one who coup'd
the bathroom, pretending

to shit or piss or wash skin
& drowned his bark, his bite
with water

the others
left to his snarl

& one of us, president
behind the only lock
the one who trumped

with our silence
with our human need

Partition

AUGUST 15TH, 1947

At the stroke of midnight, _____ achieved freedom, resulting in a
                                  country

_____ celebration. Both _____ and _____ fought for many
adjective   country   country

months to come to this agreement and now that the _____ are gone
                                                    proper noun

the _____ people celebrate their victory. "We end today a period of
    proper noun

all _____ and _____ discovers herself anew," said _____, in a
    noun   country   proper noun

public speech, to great cheers of _____. With _____'s promises of
                                  slogan   country

the security of the _____ region and its borders, _____'s citizens
                    proper noun   country

_____ to put the unfortunate events of the last few months behind
verb

them, and _____ with their new neighbors. Though millions
          verb

_____, leaders assure _____ and future prosperity alongside
past tense verb   noun

cooperation with the military. _____ people are advised to shed fear,
                               proper noun

and _____ the new _____. _____ vowed that members of all
    verb   country   proper noun

_____ are welcome in _____, but asked _____ to honor the
religion   country   religion

_____'s flag. However, if you are planning to leave for _____,
country   country

please do not forget to surrender your _____ and ration cards
                                       plural noun

(_____ and _____) at the _____ railway station. We wish you
 noun   noun   proper noun

peace and _____. _____ !
          noun   slogan

[65]

They Asked for a Map

"Nobody in India will love me."
—Cyril Radcliffe, who made the borders of Partition in less than
40 days without ever previously visiting South Asia

& so I drew them a line.

what does it mean, to partition earth?
        to cut the ocean? all the fish

wear flags on their fins.
        the flies pledge allegiance

to which bodies, rotting
        in the street, are theirs to nibble.

snowcocks nest on trees of their union
        & name themselves Indian.

fisherman cast lines
        across a liquid border

& become spies, bugging the other sides
        fauna, dragging mackerel to daylight.

kafilas clash, territorial, murderers,
        in the no man's land.

they asked for a map
        & so I drew a line

down the army, down the police
       down the guns & the bayonets.

cousins partitioned from cousins,
       mothers partitioned from child,

neighbors spearing neighbors,
       women, virgins, jumping into wells

so full with people they can't
       find water to drown.

Microaggression Bingo

White girl wearing a bindi at music festival	Friend defends drone strikes to play "devil's advocate"	Teacher still calls you "Fat-ma" on the last day of class	"But you are lucky you have something exotic to write about!"	Everyone thinks you're an expert yogi even though you can't touch your toes
Stranger calls you sexy samosa at the bus stop & then asks for your number	"I went to India once, to *find myself*."	Casting call to audition for Terrorist #7	All the actors in a movie about Egypt are white	"Oh, but you don't *really* seem Muslim."
"You're from Kashmir? I have a <rug/ sweater/ scarf> from there!"	Someone misspells both your first & last name in an email	**Don't Leave Your House For a Day - Safe**	"Oh, but I read a book by Jhumpa Lahiri once: all South Asians are *so* rich."	Editor recommends you add more white people to your story to be more relatable
Casting call to audition for Battered Hijabi Women #42	"I'm working on a story about Muslims. Could you read it & tell me what you think? I'll take you out to coffee!"	"But America is so much safer for women."	Get called a FOB & told you smell like curry	"So what's Muslim food taste like?"
"You're from the same place that M.I.A is from, right?"	"I love hanging out with your family, it always feels so *authentic!*"	The villains are wearing headscarves in yet another fantasy series	"Oh, did your parents make you wear a Hijab?"	In the 5th week of class on Bollywood a student refers to South Asia as the Middle East

My Love for Nature

All this tall grass has ruined my gold
acrylic nails & I know something's dead
just beyond my window. I grew up
with rats running my floorboards
the smell that strains from a body
caught in a trap. In the city
what little I have of an ass
is always out, a simple wind blow
from *Marilyn Monroe*–ing the street.

I promised myself I'd be naked,
here, in all this nature, but the first day
I found a tick clinging to my arm hair for dear
life & decided no way I'm exposing
my pussy to the elements. My love
for nature is like my love for most things:
fickle & theoretical. Too many bugs
& I want a divorce.

My love for the past is like my love
for most things. I only feel it when
I leave. Last week, before I was here
my uncle drove me from our city
to the suburbs & sang "Project Chick"
in the car. When we parked
he asked me to take off my shoes

& there we walked, silent, barefoot
circling the lake, trying to not step
in goose shit.

He walked in front & I trailed behind
both our hands clasped behind our backs.
He said:

> When you were my daughter,
> it was the happiest days of my life.
> I wish you would come home.

Best to stay gone, so I'm always in love.
My gold nails are fake. The floorboards
carry death. My bare feet skirt the shit.

Ghareeb

Meaning: stranger, one without a home and thus, deserving of pity. Also: westerner.

on visits back your english sticks to everything.
your own auntie calls you ghareeb. stranger

in your family's house, you: runaway dog turned wild.
your little cousin pops gum & wears bras now: a stranger.

black grass swaying in the field, glint of gold in her nose.
they say it so often, it must be your name, stranger.

when'd the west set in your bones? you survive
each winter like you were made for snow, a stranger

to each ancestor who lights your past. your parents,
dead, never taught you their language—stranger

to everything that tries to bring you home. a silver sun
& blood-soaked leaves, everything a little strange

& a little the same—like the hump of a deer on the busy
road, headless, chest propped up as the cars fly by. strange

no one bats an eye. you should pray but you're a bad muslim
everyone says. the Qur'an you memorized turns stranger

in your mouth, sand that quakes your throat. gag & ache
even your body wants nothing to do with you, stranger.

how many poems must you write to convince yourself
you have a family? everyone leaves & you end up the stranger.

Halal

the uber I step into is halal.
at least the driver tells me so.
he says, *this window is halal*

this door is halal, this floor
& we both laugh, the prayer
hung in the rearview

a minaret that calls my knees,
the closest to masjid
I have been in years.

tonight this ride is the umma
I choose, the driver's hoot
a dervish that whirls my smile.

he says:
> *I am 1% halal, 99% shaitan*
> *at least my devil is honest.*

khuda ka shukr, at least my devil
is honest: my skirt a little too short
my collarbones, ridges

for lovers' fingers to find flight.
I never dress right for any
weather, my arms a gathering of bumps

all my aunties' shame ice
the blood below my inked veins.
my knees wobble on the edge

of what I should be & what I am.
at the end of my sight I dream a world
brimming with my contradictions.

when I turn to look it disappears.
my devil quiet the days I wrap my hair
in a bouquet. but tonight, mashallah,

we are safe from his gaze in this rushed
chariot. I lace the backseat with my haram.
I trace an altar in my god's name.

Map Home

ACROSS

6 you chased after a man & after a language that don't belong to you

7 clouded by these big words, keys to the mind & the small words you collect in your palms

8 like, here: the way your parents' names, small gifts, show up in the mouths of the living

DOWN

1 he's everywhere, now that you've said no

2 & spelled your mother's name wrong for most of your life

3 despite it all, there's a path that leads to love

4 like, here: your not-dad, who could've been & if he had you wouldn't be so alone

5 but still you insist on making eye contact with pain—you insist on returning to the memories of your mother's mother

9   you need to go back & so you
    do. stay there a while in that
    room: your immigrant auntie
    watching from her bed

14 as you replay the rusted stories, age-
    wrinkled. the movies you were too
    young to see unspool on the screen

10 the country no one wants creeps
    into your every sentence

15 you're bad at goodbyes. each night you
    set a plate at dinner for the sister who
    leaves. family by another name.
    forgive her, when she walks away

11 while you force the gates open,
    one at a time. a gentle hand,
    pushing in. you can win her
    back—your childhood

16 & remember instead where you first
    learned to ride a bike, her gentle hand
    pushing you away

12 just smile wide,
    here's how to get everyone to stay

17 the wind on your face
    like the month you first met your love,
    paperclips linking in your stomach
    remember—

13 here's how to get rid of the dust.
    your home so far away. the fog
    high around your head. you can
    write the spell, you can redraw
    the map, you can fight your way
    back.

Partition

If I say the word enough I can write myself out of it:
like the driver rolling down that partition, please
again & again & a new nation springs up

in the limo, alive for a night, just one night, partition:
red lipstick smudging lines into the sand,
partition, our bodies tangled, refusing the break.

The fresh flag rolled over our naked partition,
how easy to make a word just a word, to bite its skin
with our teeth & slit. We divide & become something new.

My god partitions sunlight into many rays. They dance,
partitioned, on the sidewalk, against the trees, my skin.
My god partitions asphalt from asphalt. Each crack I dare

not step for the fury it'll cause my mother resting in her sky.
The ground partitions into what will grow & what won't.
Even nature is fractured, partitioned. I want to believe in rebirth

that what comes from death is life, but I have blood
from someone's father's father on my hands
& no memory of who died for me to be here.

Other Body

I walk throughout the day with my organs out
       the mosquitos orbit my blood.

I watch a petal open into a skirt of pink
       & think of how I waited for my first period

for years & the morning the red stain
       rippled in the toilet. How I played football

with the boys in the school park
       & my mustache grew longer

than anyone in my class.
       In my sex dreams a penis swings

between my legs, a pendulum clock
       tower puncturing my days. I watch

myself destroy the bodies of others
       wetness blooms across the sheets.

Mother, where are you? How would
       you have taught me to be a woman?

A man? Can you help me? Each day
       without you I pile questions

& whisper them to your new body,
    the earth & the grass laughs

in my face. Sometimes I laugh
    alone & for a moment forget

I was talking to you. Sometimes
    I let my grief go & my body is fully mine.

Fully alive, dancing, boy-girl
    feet pounding the ground.

National Geographic

I see my not-me on the news.
She who weds for her sweet sixteen

mosquito bites for breasts. My not-khaala's
trace her hands with mehndi, a plate

of mathai bursting at her feet. My not-khalu's
dance, pound palm to drum, stave

off monsoons. My not-abbu checks
the sheets for her blood the morning

after, brandishes the satin like a flag
his pride, singing through the town.

There's my not-me again, the one
I could've been, drowned in a burka

on her way to the market, fingering
mangos through gloves, nihari

steaming for hours at the flat shared
with my not-husbands family.

My not-me's eyes, brilliant & green
decorating the pages of western

magazines. Eyes that earn a white man
awards & showings, but eyes that stay

niqaabed in the mountains, while my not-me
rims her son's mouth with salt to trick

his belly into not-hunger.
My not-me celebrating Diwali, lights

gathered at the base of her door.
My not-me Indian, worshipping a host

of different gods, calling all their names
my not-tongue not foreign, not accented

not strange. My not-me not worried
about Taliban, but still worried about men

My not-me on the bus divided
among the passenger's hands

abdomen gutted, left on a road to die.
Still. Not-me. Alone. & not me.

WWE

Here's your cousin, in her best gold-threaded shalwaar
kameez, made small by this land of American men.

Every day she prays. Rolls attah. Pounds the keema,
at night watches the bodies of these glistening men.

Big & muscular, neck full of veins, bulging in the pen.
Her eyes kajaled, wide, glued to sweaty American men.

She smiles guilty as a bride without blood, her love
of this new country, cold snow & naked American men.

"Stop living in a soap opera" yells her husband, fresh
from work, demanding his dinner: American. Men

take & take & yet you idolize them still, watch
your cousin as she builds her silent altar to them—

her knees fold on the rundown mattress, a prayer to the pen
Her tasbeeh & TV: the only things she puts before her husband.

She covers bruises & never lets us eat leftovers: a good wife.
It's something in their nature: what America does to men.

They can't touch anyone without teeth & spit
unless one strips the other of their human skin.

Now that you're older she calls to say he hit
her again. This didn't happen before he became American.

Even now, you don't get it. But whenever it's on you watch
them snarl like mad dogs in a cage—these American men.

You know its true & try to help, but what can you do?
You, Fatimah, who still worships him?

Stank

Each morning I stitch a scowl
over my smile. Let my eyes sass
every person standing between me
& the bus stop. My eyelashes
icy. Call it *survival*. Call it *eyeliner*
so crisp it could kill a bitch.

You look prettier when you smile
says the traffic guard & I cut
out his tongue: a pet snail
slimy in my palm. Each crooked smile
that comes my way—I take all their lips
& mount them to my wall.

Ay can I get your number?
& the air sucked through my teeth
cuts the windshields open, dead
day of summer. Don't fuck with me
bitch. I'm queen of the clap back.
Thesauruses on my throne.

Got dead bodies in my closet.
Cause of death? Thirst. Cause of death?
Frostbite, burn, too hot, too cold.

Look, I'm Not Good at Eating Chicken.

& yes, my family did raise me right. Yes,
they stripped their bones & cracked them clean
open to suck. Would fight over cartilage & knuckle.
Sip the marrow's nectar from urn. Yes, I watched.
Yes, I'll teach my children the same. To savor
the sound of their teeth against bone pulling & pulling
always in search of more. But right now I'm alone
in a strange city with money in my pocket
no children waiting to be fed or taught. Meat on the bones,
skin in the trash. Joints a trap of bird & muscle
wanting to be chewed. Let me be young & disrespectful.
Let me leave my plate an unfinished slaughter.
Let me spend & eat until I, no one else, says I'm done.

Oh Pussy, The Things I've Pulled From You

clove of garlic, yellow juice, fingers
forgotten, sleeping beauties, pyrite's
many-faced shine, daffodil head in full
bloom, wind-heavy seed, blood clot, lip,
thick tongue, red name, yogurt tampon,
popcorn kernel not yet popped, blonde
hair from a roommates head, cottage
cheese discharge, house on the prairie,
dog bark & all, new couch, lost rubber,
highlighter, broom stick, brush handle,
cucumber—

you: wizard pussy, you—puss of charms,
well-read puss, uncomplaining puss, soldier puss,
miracle fruit, weathering all my experiments.

you cast your spells & the infection is gone,
you cast your spells & my body lives,
you cast your spells & another doesn't
grow inside of it, pussy of marvels,
shrine I take for granted, shrine
I don't deserve, but who blesses me
always,   always.

Partition

I pluck my ancestors eyes
from their faces
& fasten them to mine.

Widowed tree,
roads caravanned with cars
browned date palms, trampled.

The house packed
in twenty minutes, suitcase
crammed with toys & attah.

The war
no one calls war
crisps my Ullu's tongue.

He runs towards
& away while the field
—while the ghost trains

deliver bones, burnt
while I bury the stories
of my dead at the tree's base

to dig up when winter ends.

How'd Your Parents Die Again?

Again? As though I told you how the first time.
Everyone always tries to theft, bring them back out the grave.

Let them rest; my parents stay dead. Their dirge, my every
-morning's minaret. All the world's earth is my momma's grave.

The water droplet on the park's sunflower petal: her name.
I kiss every stone & it becomes my father's tomb: his grave.

They said I was too young for the funerals, so I played
dress up at home. I've never been to my daddy's grave.

My ache: two jet fuels ruining the sun's set play. The bee's
discarded wing, glazed into honey. Everywhere I look—graves.

Would I trust a God that promised me my family?
Does it matter how, if they're gone, twenty-five years, a grave

what's left of their remains? Does it matter how? There's no
place to see them again. Home is the first grave.

Super Orphan

Today, I donned my cape like a birth
certificate & jumped, arms wide into the sky.

-

Woke up, parents still
gone. Outside, the leaves yawn,

re-christen themselves as spring.

-

I know—once there was a man.
Or maybe a woman.

Let's try again: once, there was a family.
What came first?

-

What to do then, when the only history
you have is collage?

-

Today, I woke:
a king over Gotham.

The city sinning at my feet
begging to be saved.

-

The same dream again:
police running after my faceless
family with guns

my uncle leaps into a tulip
filled field, arms turning to wings
as bullets greet him.

-

Today, I woke, slop-lipped
& drunk, cards in my hand,

Joker on my chest. Today I woke
angry at the world for wanting

to make more like me.

-

Are all refugees superheroes?

Do all survivors carry villain inside them?

-

Today, I donned my cape like a birth
certificate & jumped, arms wide into the sky.

-

How else to say I am here?

A Starless Sky Is A Joy Too

ending with a line from Nikki Giovanni

If you, for a second, can put away the dead
you'll see: always the extra candy Uncle M

brought for you & your sisters
because he, too, missed your mother.

No complaints of too young & too much
sugar, the stacks of lollipops & tootsie rolls

shaped into dinner. Praise the days before
the family fled each other, everyone gathered

in the backyard, birdie zipping from racket
to racket, ice cold Cola in your Auntie P's stern

hands waiting inside, the night fading to night
fireflies sparkling the dying grill.

Even if you didn't have one, someone's door
always open, a drink ready at the table.

Their doors always open, almond oil at the table:
        older cousins who saw you at Uncle M's
burial, hair ratted in tangles. Each older girl, names
        you can't remember, dipping your strands

combing the ends & spinning tales of your beauty.
        He died & the blood family broke, spilled
like a runny egg on toast. Your aunties turned to ghost
        after they put him in the ground, flowers laid.

Orphans make family of anyone & everyone, universal
        blood. Charity child, hair always brushed, government
lunch & not enough money for the bus. All the women
        flung their doors open, neighborhood—your name

plaited tresses until they behaved. What's blood
        anyway, other than a river waiting to wake?

What's blood anyway, just a river waiting to sick.

Orphan turns strangers to mud, quakes the earth

cancer stalks each woman in your life to her grave.

You & the doctor got different definitions of family

so papers asking for bloodhistory stay empty.

Oh well. Let's put away the death waiting to happen—

it always gets into everything. It wasn't so bad, really.

Ramen seasoning flavoring your morning eggs

& sure, there was Ullu who quieted your knees to prayer

forts built with a knife as the key. & the latch

to the neighbors' barbeques, strangers lazy-susaning

you on laps & whispering: *I could be your mom if you need one.*

& yes, of course you needed one. & in the end,

you managed to get all the mothers you could ask for.

You managed to get all the mothers you asked for
& called them a different name instead—*auntie*.
Like Auntie A who dressed you up in a witch's
costume that first Halloween & took you out
when your sisters didn't want you around.
You had her all to yourself that night, riding
the bus for hours. The city yours, its alleyways
& veiny side streets unfolding at your touch. Yes,
America has failed every immigrant to enter
its harbor. The dream they came for breaks like family.
But here is the dream no one expected: her hand
to hold, the streetlights guiding your path.
This night, packed with its costumes & pretenders
& you, at the center, finding something real.

& you, at the center, finding something real:

your Auntie, a play-mom, the child she lost forgotten
    your parents laughing together on their underground date.
Hand-sewn kupre each Eid, velvet scrunchies to match.
    Your best friend's Bulgarian mom, thermometer

when you didn't have one. Your Uncle Fuzzy's Urdu, balm
    salam to every friend who came through the door
fingers in the cheese, fresh roti sizzling the pan, onions & jam.
    How their families put aside a special plate, no pork,

just for you. Marilyn's Auntie Debbie asking after you
    when she called. The America that found you alone
& opened. The doors, the windows, the strangers turned to mud
    & then sprung, again, quakes stilled, cracks filled

this kindness, this hope, which kept you alive & fighting.

The recklessness that kept you alive & fighting:
you & your sisters dangle bare brown legs over
the fire escape during winters' cold just because.
No one there to watch or tell you no.

Hot chips & burnt pasta sauce for dinner, again
three way calling boys, no auntiji to cut the line
& hiss *haram*. the nights of no curfew.
Just you, your sisters, & your own

rules to make & break: wolves, hungry
& hunting without adults, scenting your path.
three girls with no one to tell them what to do
three girls pledging allegiance to each other

three girls staking their flag *orphan* & no one
understands all the while you were quite happy.

If They Come for Us

these are my people & I find
them on the street & shadow
through any wild all wild
my people my people
a dance of strangers in my blood
the old woman's sari dissolving to wind
bindi a new moon on her forehead
I claim her my kin & sew
the star of her to my breast
the toddler dangling from stroller
hair a fountain of dandelion seed
at the bakery I claim them too
the Sikh uncle at the airport
who apologizes for the pat
down the Muslim man who abandons
his car at the traffic light drops
to his knees at the call of the Azan
& the Muslim man who drinks
good whiskey at the start of maghrib
the lone khala at the park
pairing her kurta with crocs
my people my people I can't be lost
when I see you my compass
is brown & gold & blood
my compass a Muslim teenager
snapback & high-tops gracing

the subway platform
Mashallah I claim them all
my country is made
in my people's image
if they come for you they
come for me too in the dead
of winter a flock of
aunties step out on the sand
their dupattas turn to ocean
a colony of uncles grind their palms
& a thousand jasmines bell the air
my people I follow you like constellations
we hear glass smashing the street
& the nights opening dark
our names this country's wood
for the fire my people my people
the long years we've survived the long
years yet to come I see you map
my sky the light your lantern long
ahead & I follow I follow

Notes

"For Peshawar" is in reference to the terrorist attack on the Army Public School in Peshawar on December 16, 2014. One hundred and forty-one people were killed, including one hundred and thirty-two schoolchildren between the ages of eight and eighteen.

In "Partition," "in 1946: a woman registers to vote . . . ," Laylat al-Qadr refers to one of the most powerful nights during Ramzan when the verses of the Qur'an were revealed to Prophet Muhammad. In 1947, Laylat al-Qadr fell on August 14, Independence Day for Pakistan. Ghusl refers to the Muslim ritual of washing a close relative's body before burial.

In *How We Left: Film Treatment*," the phrase Pakistan Murdabad means death to Pakistan and was used heavily during Partition to express anti-Pakistan sentiment.

The languages listed in "From" are English, Urdu, Hindi, and Punjabi, from top to bottom.

In "Haram," Astaghfirullah means I seek forgiveness from Allah. Surah means a chapter in the Qur'an.

In Western culture, owls are regarded as wise and often denote authority. In Urdu, "owl" translates to "ullu," which means "idiot."

"Partition," "It was 2000 . . ." is after Tim Seibles.

"The Last Summer of Innocence" is after Danez Smith.

"Partition," "August 15th, 1947" is after Charlotte Abotsi.

"Halal" is after Safia Elhillo. Khuda ka shukr means hallelujah.

"National Geographic" is after Kate Daniels.

Gratitude to the following journals for publishing versions of poems appearing in this book:

Academy of American Poets, *Poem-a-Day*, "WWE"

Adroit Journal, "Other Body" (published as "Mother")

Amazon *Day One,* "The Last Summer of Innocence"

BuzzFeed Reader, "Land Where My Father Died" and "100 Words for 45th's 100 Days"

Gulf Coast, "Playroom"

Indiana Review, "Old Country"

Orion Magazine, "Gazebo"

POETRY magazine, "My Love for Nature," "If They Should Come for Us," a visual collaboration of "From" with Eve Ewing, and selections of "Oil"

Prairie Schooner, "To Prevent Hypothermia"

Southern Indiana Review, "Stank"

The Lifted Brow, "National Geographic" (published as "Could've Been")

The Margins (Asian American Writers' Workshop), "For Peshawar" and "Super Orphan"

The Rumpus, "Microaggression Bingo" and "Look, I'm Not Good at Eating Chicken"

The Common, "Kal"

"*How We Left:* Film Treatment" won the Michael R. Gutterman Award in Poetry and was published in *The Best New Poets 2017* anthology. Many of these poems were in a winning manuscript for the Hopwood Award for graduate poetry at the University of Michigan.

Gratitude

I am grateful for my family, without whom I would not exist. To my sisters, Ruquia Asghar and Khudejha Asghar, for being the strongest women I know. For Aunty Kaniz and Uncle Fuzzy, who loved me when they didn't have to. For my *bajis*: Neelo, Amina, and Fauzia. And for Farhan *Bai*.

For my parents, Ghazalah Kausar Asghar and Ghulam Malik Asghar. I only wish for your love. I hope I make you proud.

For Dark Noise, my bloodriders. You make me proud to walk beside you. For Nicholas Ward, who read every draft of every poem.

To my mentors: Tarfia Faizullah, Jamaal May, Thalia Field, Catherine Imbriglio, Besenia Rodriguez, Rachel McKibbens, Krista Franklin, Ross Gay, Patricia Smith, Aimee Nezhukumatathil, and Douglas Kearney. Thank you for your belief and for pushing me to be better.

Thank you to the One World Team: Nicole Counts, Christopher Jackson, and Victory Matsui. A special thanks to Nicole Counts, who held me through every step of this book. This book would not have been possible without you.

To my friends, who looked over this book with so much attention and painstaking detail: Danez Smith, Phillip B. Williams, Kevin Coval, Ray McDaniel, Nate Marshall, Franny Choi, Aaron Samuels, Hieu Nguyen, and Jamila Woods. Thank you to 3Arts Entertainment, to my manager, Jermaine Johnson, and my agents, Rachel Kim and Richard Abate. Thank you to my lawyers at Frankfurt Kurnit Klein & Selz, Amy Nickin and Michael Williams.

To my kin, for keeping me strong: Sam Bailey, Vince Martell, Teodora Kaltcheva, Jaspreet Kaur, Nabila Hossain, Rehan Siddiqui, Becca Evans, Marilyn Paschal, Safia Elhillo, H. Melt, Sarah Coakley, Angel Nafis, Hanif Abdurraqib, Kaveh Akbar, Safiyah Sinclair, Mo Browne, Sam Sax, Cam Awkward-Rich, Malcolm Shanks, Eve Ewing, Jayson Smith, VyVy Trinh, Laura Brown-Lavoie, Jess X. Chen, Sarah Kay, Phil Kaye, Amina Sheikh, Ceci Pineda, José Olivarez, Marco Lambooy, Jasmin Panjeta, Jonah Mixon-Webster, Raych Jackson, Kush Thompson, Dimress Dunnigan, Britteney

Kapri, Jacqui Germain, Amy Sewick, Mina Zachkary, and Adam Kiki-Charles. Thank you to Don Share, Kyle Dargan, and Hayan Charara for believing in my work, even when I struggled to believe. Thank you to Kundiman, to the Poetry Foundation, Vermont Studio Center, Millay Colony, University of Michigan, and New Harmony Writers Workshop for giving me the time, support, and space I needed to complete this book.

To everyone else whom I have met, who has influenced me, and who has been there, thank you.

About the Author

FATIMAH ASGHAR is a nationally touring poet,
performer, educator, and writer. She is the writer
of *Brown Girls,* an Emmy-nominated web series that
highlights friendships between women of color. She
is a member of Dark Noise and a 2017 Ruth Lilly and
Dorothy Sargent Rosenberg Poetry Fellow.

fatimahasghar.com
browngirlswebseries.com
Twitter: @asgharthegrouch
Instagram: @asgharthegrouch

About the Type

This book was set in Dante, a typeface designed by Giovanni Mardersteig (1892–1977). Conceived as a private type for the Officina Bodoni in Verona, Italy, Dante was originally cut only for hand composition by Charles Malin, the famous Parisian punch cutter, between 1946 and 1952. Its first use was in an edition of Boccaccio's *Trattatello in laude di Dante* that appeared in 1954. The Monotype Corporation's version of Dante followed in 1957. Though modeled on the Aldine type used for Pietro Cardinal Bembo's treatise *De Aetna* in 1495, Dante is a thoroughly modern interpretation of that venerable face.